SET DOWN HERE

SET DOWN HERE

Lolette Kuby

Brandylane Publishers, Inc.
Richmond, Virginia

copyright 2002 by Lolette Kuby
All rights reserved.
Printed in the United States of America.

ISBN 1-883911-49-4

Cover design consultant: Rod Nash, R.G.D.

More Praise for *Set Down Here*

"Lolette Kuby is a passionate and tenacious poet. Language, too, is fiercely loved—a Kuby simile branches into similes that don't rest on their ingenuity but keep topping themselves. She's a pleasure and a comfort, often the powerful flashlight you need in a dark wood; you'll be glad she was set down here."

Bonnie Jacobson,
Stopping for Time and *In Joanna's House*

"Kuby affords a rich and varied choice, poems of wit, of passion, of sheer force..."

Frank Polite
Letters of Transit, Flamingo, and Hyde,
and Pushcart Prize winner

"...these poems turn the observed moment from sorrow to a conclusion of openness where joy, compassion and hope emerge unexpectedly. This voice is tough and fair; it also believes in the fact and purpose of a human soul. Throughout one receives the clear impression of a voice that has earned the right to pronounce the tales it tells. Would there were more."

Nicholas Ranson, Editor, bits press

For Jordan and Alexandra

TABLE OF CONTENTS

PART ONE: FOLLOWING DAYS

When He Dies	2
Walk on the Night Beach	3
...And Four to Go	4
Elegy for Max	6
Sentimental Moon	8
Leaving	9
Death Wish	10
How It Was	11
To Each	14
Walking in the Woods with My Mother	15
The Coffee House at Christmas	16
Following Days	17
At Three O'Clock in the Morning	18
My Mother's Letters	19
The Last Obit	20
Calendar Art	21
The Separation	23
Thirty Years Later	25
Moving On	27
Windfalls	28
The Grandmothers	29
The Bad Child	30
Playing Blackjack with Black Jack	31
The Leaving	33
The Good Night	34
Your Daughter's Eyes	36
Touchpoint	37
On Hearing of My Daughter's Intended Divorce	39
Subway Tracks	41
Beaches	42
Glass Houses	43

Helen	44
The Day Sleeper	45
In Line	46
The Fox Jumps Over the Fence	47
I Have This Here Big Sleeping Bag	48

PART TWO: WHITE SMOKE

Down in the Andes	52
At an Exhibit of Holocaust Art	54
Packing Light	56
Waking at Midnight	58
Condolences	59
White Smoke	61
Written on Christmas Eve	62
Turning Out	63
Pas de Deux	64
Any Day	66
Where Marty Is	67
Regarding a Deaf Child	68
Spaces	69
Learning to Love	70
No More Passion Plays	71
Procession	73
Choosing Your Genre	75
At Two O'Clock in the Night	76
Young Soldier, Crisp and Clean	77
Halfway House	78
The Appointed Place	79
Fake Flowers	80
Come Join Me	81
Iniquity	82

PART THREE: SET DOWN HERE

Set Down Here	84

PREFACE

Much as I love to write, I dislike writing *about* my work. Yet I sympathize with and share readers' curiosity to catch a glimpse backstage. So I will say a bit here about the kind of poems I admire and attempt to write, and about the generative process.

So often poets are asked where poems come from—what puts the key in the ignition, what makes the engine kick over and when does the vehicle reach its destination? My answer I'm afraid will be very similar to those of other poets. A poem may come from a feeling of obligation to an occasion—a birth or a death or even a sunset: "I *should* write about that sunset," I tell myself. But nagging at the occasion won't produce a poem, at least not a good one, unless the occasion nags back with an insistence other than obligation. A poem may come from a purely abstract idea; if the idea is alive it pushes and I begin to pull. A poem may come from an experience, from an image, from a string of words that seem to enter my head out of nowhere. I collect all of these on scraps of paper (including the legendary cocktail napkin), and this collection comprises my dark room. Later, I find that one or two have begun to develop as if all on their own. As I work on these, I find that some get brighter and clearer, that is, they're dynamic—I was going to say "dramatic," except that drama implies a situation, whereas pure thought can be the drama of a poem.

The poem propels me to its end—a combination of unconscious mind and the internal associations found within language itself when one starts to play with it—as, I hope, it will propel the reader; I have to *feel* something when I write it and then again when I read it.

I feel exhilarated when I finish a poem. But when I am wise enough to let the poem rest—the longer the better—when I reread it, it is either still fresh and provocative, or a leaden lump. The latter, of which there are far more than the former, go into the trash. Laboring over a dead poem is like putting makeup on a corpse.

And when exactly is a poem finished? In one sitting you can get something onto a page that looks like a poem and which often has much in it that remains in the final draft. Poems that seem promising I gather in a file called "PIPS"—Poems In Progress. But a poem is never finished. Weeks, months, even years after I regard a poem as "done," I change something in it. "Done," to me means temporarily done with; it means I am satisfied enough to submit the poem to the world.

I can give you an example of how some of what I have said applies to "Where Marty Is." The poem's muse was an occasion—the death of Rosie, an old high school friend, of breast cancer. I started by putting down memories—flashes of images that came immediately to mind. I had no idea where the poem would go, and as you'll see, it took an unexpected direction. As I recollected Rosie, I thought of what rabbis often say at funerals to give comfort to the living—that the departed will live on in memory. I have always remained uncomforted. If memory is the only form life takes after death, it is a sadly skeletal form. For who knows even a fraction of the life of even the one we loved most? The person himself, who occupies his life breath by breath, is not *aware* of what is going on in the infinitude of complexities that comprise it. So, my thoughts continued, if something survives after death that can be called life, it must be alive of itself; it must transcend the combined memories of all of us. Thus the poem discovered where it wanted to go, which was to the indestructible—to Rosie's soul.

After I had written that poem, it came to me that the poem would be stronger if the persona were a male. So I said goodbye to Rosie and invented Marty. Now I had to make up "memories." What had been real became completely fictive. And Marty's death by cancer of the brain seemed appropriate for a poem that rejects memory as the form afterlife takes. The soil "knows" that matter is indestructible; Marty's muscle and bone have become it. His soul's continuation is more mysterious—less local and less locatable. It is found in the choirs of birds. And blending the two images—soil and song—further suggests the union of matter and spirit: the songs of birds somehow depend upon the bird ingesting what the soil brings forth, and what the soil brings forth is transformed into song. Of course no analysis of a poem, including the poet's, "owns" the poem.

A prose writer once wisely said, "You have 500,000 bad words in you. Get as many out of yourself as quickly as you can." Since the entire oeuvre of poets, even epic poets, rarely approaches this number, a poet has to expel far fewer, but the definition of "bad" is far more stringent. I must admit I have a prejudice against what I call the laundry list or the grab bag—poems crammed with "things." Poets are lucky that books of poems aren't movie fodder; poets don't have to write with one eye cocked toward the big screen that must be filled with things. The benefit of "things" in poems is not to supplant ideas but to authenticate them, not to eradicate vision but to intensify it. The burden of a poem should not be a load of objects, but a signification, a foundational meaning, a reification. I expect a good poem, aside from the skills of language and rhythm it displays, to gratify an exploration into its psychology and philosophy. In other words, I want in a good poem what I want in a good human being—a happy union of body, mind, and spirit.

After reading a truly good poem, you enter a silence—a moment composed of inner quietness and awakening. If you do not enter that silence, either you or the poem is not ready. There is a short way of saying everything I have said here: Fiction points to itself; poems point beyond themselves: prose ends at the word; poetry begins with it.

ACKNOWLEDGEMENTS

Elegy for Max, *Poet Lore*; Death Wish, *Prairie Schooner*; How it Was, *Farmer's Market*; To Each, The Last Obit, *Light Year'85*; Pas de Deux (Publ. as Duo for Voice and Body), *Salome*; Helen, *Scape*; In Line, *Proteus*; Halfway House, And Four to Go, *In Enormous Water*: The Good Night, *Nightsun*; The Grandmothers *Voices of Cleveland;* Walking in the Woods with my Mother, *Whiskey Island*.

Part I
Following Days

WHEN HE DIES

When you hear about his death it may be
the climax of autumn, and you pruning
dead branches from a flaming oak, the air
golden and pungent with fresh wood, homey
as bread baking; or it may be August,
and you lying on the grass on a star-
filled night, when the telephone summons you
from the whorl of planets; or it may be
you have just reached your door, soaked by springtime's
storm, with lightning thick as your arm striking
around you, when the letter arrives. Years
later you could answer, *I remember
the moment perfectly. I was right there
doing exactly that.* But you will hear
during a moment unmemorable
as the drone of traffic—the announcement
only epilogue to an old story.
It will be like the non-event of his
birth into an overpopulated
household in an overpopulated
planet—life sailing by and the water
closing behind.

WALK ON THE NIGHT BEACH

Low tide.
Long long reach of sand, then spindrift
far away as snowblown Christmas.
Indentations of very small toes—
footprints of, I'd guess, a three-year old.
One bright star, far, perhaps, as thirty years,
between humpbacked clouds beckons.

These, I think, are important thoughts.

The sandpipers are sleeping.
The seagulls are sleeping.
Where do they sleep?
How many things sleep where
I don't know where. I used to know
where my children slept.
Two neat little bedrooms,
under comforters printed with stars
and clouds.

These are important thoughts,
having taken a long long time
to be not complaints.

... AND FOUR TO GO

One for the Money ...

I inspect you closely, all parts perfect,
ten fingers, ten toes—not yet of this world
and yet the harbor of three generations
of living women.

I worry about strontium ninety,
check the passage to the fire escape,
recall the headline of an infection
in a nursery, recall the Lindbergh
case; nightmare fantasies to scare away
the image of an old woman, your death
just decades away.

Between the buzz of the maternity
ward, I drift into semi-sleep while sunlight
flows slowly from the east to the west wall,
and waken to moonlight on white blankets,
white curtains, white floor,
hushed, leisurely, calm as snowfall.

Two for the Show ...

Nine. So soon. Your long legs lengthened by skates.
Newly skinned knees. Your ribbons fly as though
a timid rider dropped the reins. You shout,
Mama, it's time! Then the party, prizes,
games, the ritual wish, every candle
with one breath.

Wait a minute! Stay, my clock! You push me
from behind. Ahead stands only the frail
breakwall of grandmothers.

Three to Get Ready . . .

In your closet an outgrown party dress
like a becalmed sail. All spring you queried
mirrors for a hairdo that would age you.
Decided short, like the daguerreotype
girl on the mantel. Before college
you met her, puzzled that this was the one
in the silver frame.

Her eyes looked past you as they would a tree,
a wall. On me they stopped the way the hands
of a great clock stop on a tick then move
ahead two minutes at a time. She turned
to my mother, begging the promised rock
candy on a string.

Bye, great-grandmother, you say, not knowing
what to say, I'll see you. I say, Goodbye,
grandma, not knowing what to say, I'll write.
Goodbye, Ma, my mother says, Wednesday,
I'll bring the candy.

ELEGY FOR MAX

It was like waking up one morning
and being told the Terminal Tower is gone.
No earth tremor, no violent explosion,
simply gone. Not there anymore.
Nothing to shake the populace up
(except for a few with offices inside.
Mine wasn't). I walk by it
a half-dozen times a year, maybe less,
but I never walk by it unaware.
Half its offices are empty. It straddles
a great subterranean maze
of railroad tracks where Cleveland, in its heyday,
was the country's crossroads.
Kids in its observation tower
still get their first perspective of reality
as a toy: cars smaller than the smallest model,
people comically diminished, the flung spitball
falling into nowhere. It captures your imagination,
this building, with its caverns webbing underground
and its flagpole fifty-four stories up, clanging.
In some ways the announcement of your death
was someone saying the Terminal Tower is gone.

II

A ship.
Why do I think of you as a great structure?
The Terminal Tower. A ship.
Is it your hulk?
Your poor heart carried a big weight.
No, not that. At least, not only that. I'll get to it.
What ship? The *Queen Elizabeth*?
Too elegant. There were no classy cabins
in you. A Mississippi houseboat? Too homey,

too sentimental—banjoes and booze and
laundry in magnolia breezes (though you could belt out
lowdown and dirty blues, down in the Flats
where they paid you in drinks).
A Battleship? Never. Your big guns
were always pointed at your hold. A ship
something like a whaling ship
something like a slave ship
unsleek, unseaworthy, taking the waves
heavily, with cumbersome rolls,
a ship like the sea's Wailing Wall
with a crazy captain on deck
and high in the crow's nest
a speechless Billy Budd.

Your niece asked, Do you think he knew
how many loved him?
No, he didn't know. Or knew
the way a bird, caught in a hurricane,
knows there is a tree somewhere
rooted to receive him, or knew
the way a ship cracking on a shoal
knows there is a lighthouse searching the water
and warning fog horns
and the people of the village standing on the shoreline
calling to the wreck of the Maxwell Levey.

SENTIMENTAL MOON

Like music
it reservoirs old loves.
Play *Melancholy Baby.*
Play the lullabies
of a looney tune mother
filling your babyhead
with a different moon
at every window.

The next year collected moons
like balls of mercury
to one bright tale.
And the year after that
we moved. *The postman said,
Moon, jump in my sack,*
and the milkman and the van man
hauled the lonely moon to the faithful child.

You've moved again,
not far as the road lies,
in good weather
only an eight hour drive.

How white and silken
it floats tonight,
full of the strains
of love's sweet lies.

And beyond it another moon,
and beyond it another

farther than the light
of your years, or even mine,
has yet arrived.

LEAVING

He died like a gentleman,
all dressed up in a pin-striped suit and a tie,
shodden and shaved, stretched out
on a flowered bedspread
in a Haitian hotel room, pinned to his lapel a note
like a kindergarten boy's mittens or excuse from mother,
just cold when the detective found him.

He disappeared a year ago
leaving his wife,
all his money, the power of attorney and a note.
One day he was across the breakfast table from her,
the next, he wasn't. That's all.

What the second note said
she won't disclose. The first said,
don't follow.

DEATH WISH

When I die, I wish that you would not inter
me, but lay me on the rim,
near water, wishfully, water
with a tide, sucking its lips in, snoring:
it will remind me of Jim. Turn me
face up as though stargazing,
or moonstruck, a lover
reliving the night before.

Or lay me on my side, hand propping my head,
as though learning the worm's world,
the occupations of ants. Or spread me
on park grass where kids carry on
and an old bum, believing me kindred,
believing me chafed
by the sobering sun
stoops down to share or beg a draft.

Lay me down in the sun
but let it not scorch me

Lay me down in the rain
but let it not melt me

Let insects roam over
but let them not in me

Then let me get up and go home.

HOW IT WAS

Not much to it,
one day ended and the next begun
and each day we did what came along,
like livin out a set plan, same as always—
like schoolin; you keep goin and learnin this and that,
whatever's put in front of you,
until you get to where the certificate says you're done;
or like getting married: dances and socials until
a certain person gets inside your eyes, then one day
seein what the church is for,
then doin what feels good until your family's born—
not havin to think much about what's next.
And that's how it was the time of the big rain.
Everyone tickled silly at first. Too late for the lettuce,
but the corn lifted up its face and every little yellow
mouth drank up full. Winter wheat'd be a bumper
if it kept on. The worms and snails and slugs,
which'd shrivelled to strings and knots,
must have been crazy happy and started mating with a purpose
that kept 'em goin day and night, cause you couldn't
set down foot without squashin two at once. The town
kids ploshed in puddles and even the grown folk
walked slow as Guernseys from their car
to their porch, and some stood with their arms outstretched
like a prayin Indian, with their palms facing
the sky. Not an umbrella or a see-through bonnet
in sight. By Wednesday, though, everything was back
to normal—raincoats and runnin inside and TV watchin.
By Wednesday next, the housepainters and golfers
were growlin hard, but the fishermen were bundled
in slickers and grinnin away, and the farmers sayin
it would make up good for the April drought.
By the end of week three, the people from Environment
were on Oprah and Donahue explainin

how intelligent Mother Nature was
replenishin the water table from last summer's
near zero precipitation, tryin to get the people whose
rec room furniture was floatin around to see the greater good.
About then, it's my birthday, and my sons
and daughters and their kids come over to my house,
which sets up on a high point of my land
(because you can't plant crops on peaks),
and after the birthday cake, moister than my wife
wanted, and the candles, hard to keep lit long enough
for me to blow them out, I tell my idea
about leavin. Jack, he's a carpenter, and Marie
are dumbfounded. "Leave everything and just go?
"Either that," I say, "or . . ." and I point to the fifty
gallon aquarium with the blue bubbles and the fish
swimmin in and out of little castles and in between
plastic trees.
Jimmy gets the idea right away, and after talkin back
and forth and back to what everyone knew in the first
place, all but Thomas, who owns a sports equipment
store and sells tackle and bait and wilderness outfits,
says OK. But how?
It's a long ways 'tween thinkin and gettin,
and since Terry Pond and Osaga Creek overflew
the road nothin on wheels was rollin outta here.
Me and Jack go outside to think and as soon as we see
the big pile of lumber that was to be my new barn,
we smile at each other. "First thing tomorrow?" "Yep."
It took two weeks and by then the only things
I could see was my house and the tops of trees
and telephone poles. What Jack and me built
looks more like a barn than a boat
but it floats, and the whole family piles on,
though none of us is that gleeful. Then I get the idea
to put down the gangplank for a day before takin off
for dryer parts, and when we do, the gangplank stands
right up out of the water instead of dangling down,

like the end of it landed on a good upright rock.
All day cows and horses and pigs
come floatin down the water and heavin theirself
up onto the gangplank, with cats and squirrels
and rabbits hangin onto them, and fleas and lice and
caterpillars hangin onto them. And that's how it was—
one day and the next, just doin what came along.

TO EACH

Some people fight him.
In the morning you see them
With scabrous legs and crooked finger bones
Bits of scale or skin under their nails.

Some people play possum
Hold still, stand stiff
He circles and sniffs around them
You can smell his odor on them.

Some people try to please him
Offer a leg or a hunk of breast
But he knows they know
It's organ meat he likes best.

Some people hide in the long-ago past
But he knows the toothless smile
The blabber, the innocent eyes
Are only a disguise.

And some people leap on his back
With a twist of hemp or razor spurs
And force him to ride them
Through the white gauze and the dark funnel and the
                                        pores of stones

WALKING IN THE WOODS WITH MY MOTHER

About two miles in, through crimson and gold
rich as top milk, *more valuable than jewels*,
my mother said, wishing we were the kind
who could hold hands, link arms. We hardly talked,
except she sighed how beautiful it was,
and I said, yes, and she recited
the Ninety First Psalm, she'd lullabied
herself with during radiation
last year, its lines of vengeance excised.
Walking with my mother in the woods
the reticence of trees justified ours,
and their companionable stiffness.

THE COFFEE HOUSE AT CHRISTMAS

It used to be poultry and fish, stuffy
walkups over stores, synagogues—strange
square letters still fade off walls—then hippie.
Now it is arts and crafts and veggie
restaurants. Every city has some place
like this, where it all comes together—
Mercedes, rusted Fords, Harley Davidsons.
In summer, chess players ponder under
poor starved sidewalk trees, twinkling now with lights
for Christmas. Tame sparrows peck baklava,
ruffle the ground like living leaves. I drive

thirty miles to steam my soul on mocha-java,
drawn by something different that seems
to happen here, beyond the mistletoe
and wreaths, the *hari krishnas* entering
with the wind, the space left undisturbed
around the Yogi. Need here appears
on scraps of notebook paper thumbtacked
to the walls. Yet the clock here, too, feels
its own face over and over, and look!

across from me a baby crawls on top
of the table. Be careful, she will topple off
the edge! Watch! She will spill boiling coffee
on herself! Look!
She is eating the flowers!

FOLLOWING DAYS

Before death and taxes,
before the knowledge
that my name
did not name me,
days came white on white,
bright figures on bright ground.
Days chattered up organ grinder's
arms, tipped hats and smiled,
and I didn't notice the bones
in the comical whiskered face
but tossed my whole estate
into the jangling tambourine and followed
past boundaries of familiar space.
Days paused at curbs to be robbed
of apples. Days took my picture—worth
the enormous quarter to climb
the pony of my cowboydom—proof
of the incredible boy
to the inconceivable man.
And when days sailed off,
each spun out behind its back
the day to follow
like kite string for my hand.

AT THREE O'CLOCK IN THE MORNING

At three o'clock in the morning we're
always fat and have arthritic toes.

At six we're skinless giant embryos
pushing through the hourglass of sandy morning.

By seven, the love that never was backed
into a corner of the mind, we take

solace in coffee, and almost smile
like John Denver into our sugarless

raisins and wheat, behind our heads a too
glorious horizon of Alps and sky.

We're thankful when the engine turns without
a sputter to churn us workward. Something.

If only that first cervical hourglass
issued us old, and we cranked through ennui

and disease toward a distant youth, then we
could chant, *Everything passes.* But the best

is now, is this, and our bones like turnstiles
creak ever more heavy on their hinges.

MY MOTHER'S LETTERS

My mother charmed in her orthography.
Her letters leaned, slim and indubitable,
to whisper in your ear, or plant
a modest kiss beside your mouth.
Zeroes floated above mysterious *i*'s,
y's, looped gracefully as a chiffon scarf,
would tantalize a eunuch. Wherever
she thought, you obediently toddled
after. Dejected by the period,
the *love*, the knotted sibilant
and final flourish of *Sally*,
you'd circle back and sniff the route again.
One day you think, *She must be writing
on a train,* but no trip mentioned. Five years
before her death, the *l*'s arrived vertiginous,
the *t*'s vacant of their crossbars, the *y*'s incontinent.

THE LAST OBIT

The funeral of Lorne H. Weeks
of Kensington on the Cove
was held on Sunday afternoon
January 2, 1983
at the Davidson Funeral Home.
The service was conducted
by the late Reverend J.R. Squires.
A solo, "Beautiful Garden of Prayer,"
was sung by the late Mrs. Sande Clark.
The choir sang "In the Sweet Bye and Bye,"
to the organ of the late Mrs. Fern Causely.
Pallbearers were the late David Barglobe,
Brian Moss, Miller Weeks, and Doctor
High B. Tidesmon. Flowerbearers were
the late Carmen Woodside, Allen Weeks,
Grant McDonald, and Michael Mahem.
Interment was in the

CALENDAR ART

Your home was never a place like this,
yet the tea-cozy house and the hug of hills
are familiar as the gait of your father,
the lines on your mother's forehead.
One of the featureless figures is yourself.

    I

The pond a solid sky where skaters carve
zodiacs of their own invention, where death
cannot enter the white of hills, more comforter
than snow, your limbs, long and lithe and unweathered.

    II

The season flips and your young body
floats in a stew of lilies and minnows,
remembering its buoyancy. Fishermen
recover their timing—a contentment of waiting.

    III

Now you row the whole circumference of the sky.
Your mother appears in the doorway
like light after rain on the green gauze hills.
Your father in the fields is docile as rock.

    IV

The farm is tight and safe,
under a quilt of leaves, the good harvest
bundled and pickled and canned. Beyond
the hills there is only distance.

Distance is where meteors shower,
where fireflies burn out, where stars fall...
It is original in each of us, the sin
that calls the child to where stars fall.

You remember
the skitter of leaves, the groaning
of bullfrogs, crickets fiddling to frenzy.

THE SEPARATION

The carpenter left his West Virginia hills
to climb high icy scaffolds in Ohio,
married a rich lady, raised Arabians
on her Gates Mills estate outside Cleveland,
corrupted her son, made fifty-two thousand
a year working with his hands on rooftop
discotheques. His gnarled, bionic hands excited her.

Ten years separated from his down-home folk,
who owned their dirt-poor farms till dirt became gold,
owned all the trees in West Virginia until
a single tree, well-girthed, could bring more thousands
than a year of honest West Virginia work,
and who never did learn how to play for higher
stakes than home-canned pickles at Saturday's bazaar.

This weekend, crossing borders like illicit
love, he rides backroads to his grandma's shack
crumbled into scrub outside the lumber camp,
becomes hillbilly scrawnier, more bearded
and red-haired as evening and the hills close in.

Sunday, the narrow church in the hills fills
with the old, on whom flies settle like disease,
with long-necked women and skinny boys
and yellow-jackets darting between them
and the rafters. Afterward, cousins shyly
give their hands, "This here is Margaret's son,"
his password, and ask him home for Sunday supper
to handbuilt one-floor houses or trailers
landscaped with dwarf junipers and marigolds.

In their sons, gawky, silent, he sees how he
must have been, his birthright in their downcast eyes.

Schooldays, the sons walk uphill miles of dreaming.
September's gold falls quiet on their heads,
swirls on the ground like the whisper of hooves
after they have passed. One might wish for him
the innocence and faithfulness he left. He
wants no part of either what he lost or what he sold.

THIRTY YEARS LATER
(for Eunice)

It is an autumn afternoon,
late autumn, late afternoon,
November, almost winter.
Winter if you judge by yesterday
when sleet fell sharp
as beaks, on your windshield.
But today it is seventy degrees, the joke
about Cleveland weather proved . . .
just wait ten minutes . . . and you
are sitting on some steps
smoking a cigarette (this is when
you used to smoke) and you flick it away
and watch it scurry under a drift
of brown leaves (for it *was*
November, though warm as May).
This is before your aneurism,
your son's cancer, your husband's death,
your several lovers, all
wielding a baton over you,
muscular, demanding harmony, demanding
perfection, the baton so slim though,
so delicately held between two fingers,
like a lady sipping tea, but the other hand
a raised claw, a clutch of time,
an insistent measure.
You always hated your hands, so naked,
so big knuckled and blunt, too large
to hang off slim wrists, an old woman's
hands, fitting now, earned now
by more than the span of keys
and countless rehearsals. Weather.
One wants to play with it, to say
Whether? Whither? Whither goest thou,

old friend? Like weather goest thou,
whether you count or not, like wind
goest thou, like woodwind, will or not.
But we *will* play with it, catch
its two notes, chirp chirp, major and minor,
upbeat and downbeat. Whither?
Wither? . . . Wait ten minutes.

MOVING ON

You died when death was deeper than Sheol,
deep as neverbeing. Memory would
preserve you, the rabbi said.

Six years have dulled your red hair, drabbed your eyes
to blue stone. I have not yet removed you
from my rolodex.

I have come to believe that death is not
final. So you have merely moved on,
just as my mother moved

so long ago to California,
just as my lover moved to another
woman, just as my child

moved from the sweet-smelling infant who found
sleep in the hollow of my shoulder
and the tiny feet that took one

tentative step at a time.

WINDFALLS

There has been too much of past, too many
voids filled with successes that failed
in the long run. Doors opened and slammed,
and it isn't the crash of another
slamming that transfixes me on the threshold
now. A woman sighed, *But I wouldn't want
to be twenty again, would you?* Yes!
Oh, yes! Incredulous, she went on sure
about a dry twig's cracking clean and quick,
and a green twig's painful bending and bending.
And of course that's true about an old twig
breaking into kindling, into something
altogether different, and about
the green twig snapping back into itself
again and again. But, yes, I would choose
to be that age that predates knowing.
I don't mean knowing that anticipation
surpasses the event, or that some trees
even in Eden grow grotesquely, or that
the worm invades the fruit from its flower—
those balanced truths Eden can accommodate,
and the young planter, the one I would be,
plots and fertilizes and tills and reaps
and then rethinks it all to do it
next time differently. It's the old planter
who suddenly knows that all the sweetest
apples have been windfalls. Then the twig browns
and the gates to Eden close.

THE GRANDMOTHERS

This is the time of the forgiveness
of grandmothers, not Hallmark's grandmothers,
the grandmothers, with dog-ear breasts,
who offer birthday pennies from beaten
leather coin purses with metal teeth,
while the mothers are off kicking up heels
under blue lights or screaming their own scream
down dark alleys.

The grandmothers are dead ten years but still
bite through dust with ill-fitting porcelains,
still beam vixen eyes through dreams, but can
not catch the little mouses of joy, who
have started to leave their holes, who have started
to chirp and to eat.

So let us put the grandmothers to rest.
Let us imagine them stirring a kettle
of barley soup, flesh under arms swaying
like udders; or pink and sweating over
a scrub board, or straining in the wind toward
high laundry ropes, earthlings praying to sons'
gyrating pajamas, to daughters' slim
flowered dresses

Let us remember, when their bodies
dangled at the end of eighty years,
the time you gripped her arm to help her down
the path, and felt, under the slip of flesh,
bird bones, kitten bones. And on her cheeks
two long idle tears like the parallel
tracks of generations.

THE BAD CHILD

You might have known when her colic
pierced your dreams, no cradle or breast
could exorcise, and later when
she taunted a mother's mellowed
wisdom or waltzed beyond reach
of the useful slap. You might have known.
But mostly she walked inside your days
like a flower girl, scattering
healing noises and fragile kisses,
making your life a glowing bridal.
So you forgot how bad a child
she was, forgot until the naughty,
the incorrigible girl, turned
your clothing inside out and stole
away your shoes, and hung your mirrors
with rags, and locked herself
in her room and plucks with impunity
from their constellations
the orderly stars.

PLAYING BLACKJACK WITH BLACK JACK

1.
He twirls his patent leather mustache,
but he is blond and fair of face
as Robert Redford
and friendly as a Panda Bear.
"Play?"
He smiles and juts his handsome chin
toward the deck.
"Poker? Gin?"
I blush and shake my head,
flattered I attracted him.
"My daddy taught me only Blackjack."
"Name your stakes."

2.
Easy with him already, I quip,
"Low. Unless I can pay with plastic."
He's all grin: "Nope—
It's biodegradables I like—
what comes up green."
I sit down with him,
not telling
I'm daddy's little Blackjack
champ.

3.
On the table, by his hand
my wristwatch blinks the minutes.
My necklace with the silver heart
huddles in a heap beside my car keys.
I stay at twenty; he picks up twenty-one.
I draw at fifteen, I draw a seven.
But any minute now I know
my star will shift
to winner's heaven.

4.
My ATM card's on the table,
and a scrap of paper with my secret
number. "Daddy," I pray,
"Oh, come on, lucky star!"
He offers gently, "One last chance?
Strip Blackjack
Winner take all?"

5.
I count his clothes:
beltless pants, a shirt,
no tie, no sign of undershirt—
seven. I count up mine—with hairclips
and pantyhose—ten!

6.
I sit with my legs
pressed tightly together,
my arms folded tightly
over my breasts.
I shiver.

7.
"One hand more," he urges,
"Double or nothing . . . "
"But . . .?" I begin.
He smiles,
"The skin.
The skin."

THE LEAVING

I dreamed you left as a great brown bear,
grace in matter loping out toward the horizon
of the tundra until you disappeared
beyond the arc of earth; the semi-circle
closed behind you like water over a flung stone.
In reality you are still dying.

To me your first thirty years are stories—
a boyhood of lessons in where not to touch,
a boyhood that sat in the courtyard of shame
under the tent of a urinated sheet
gathering rage, gathering the cruelty of nuns
to fling at God.

Your dying contains my other dead men: a grandfather
with big fists, whose death by rotting
was a limping after the amputated leg; a shapeless
father, at the end shapeless as his blanket,
except where it tented over the lingering stout
refusal of the penis.

I am relieved not to witness the last month
of your body—becoming bones, needing to be turned,
raking back and forth through morphine, leaving so slowly
while you make peace. During the agony
you come upon faith—grace in matter, secreted
within, redeemed from infancy.

THE GOOD NIGHT

Night is soft
Night touches night like the folds of an accordion
Night pours into night
like the long note of an oboe

Days fracture
Days break into words
skim surfaces, stir
muddy mispopulated depths
ask questions one is supposed to answer

Night hums from the secret places of grass
Night loves night
like the brothers in the halls of Gesthemene
Night gathers to night
like drops of mercury

taking you with them

Alarmed, you struggle toward days
begin circling the bonfire of days
begin twisting tongue into syllables
naming things, parts, until days
lengthen like arctic Julys

Try to stay in days, day after day
Forget the inside of the robin's egg
the eardrum of the conch

The September sun bites like a horsefly
bloodies the outlines of the departure of geese
Days are for geese, for those infallibles
who sweep their path as they go
arrive at old place with new time
to begin

Tonight you must outdistance them
like a wind at the end of October
like a prediction of rain

YOUR DAUGHTER'S EYES

Your daughter has the eyes of an animal,
your mind's dove-colored fawn,
or the cow in the grassy field
Gautama saw himself repeated in,
eyes at the instant of waking.

You may see such eyes in zoo animals, too,
so different from their day-long
boredom and suspicion, if you sneak
under the gate at break of dawn and become
the very first human.

Have you seen the eyes of a wolf cub
caught in a trap? That deepest, brownest
suffering you may see in your daughter's eyes
after you once again pry her life apart,
and her needle-teeth pierce your wrist.

TOUCHPOINT

This, then, is how the integuments cohere,
though the spirit breaks aloft
for its habitation, we cohabitate
in a muscle of will. *I do, I will,*
broke sweetly on the tongue
and the wine glass under the heel.
This or nothing.

New fractures are mended
by old vows
the only fluxless sphere
the word
hangs holy over the head
turns upon itself,
returns,
no taking it back.
The word
said times ago
redolent with connotation
now denotes,
no getting around it,
generates tangible replicas:
an anniversary
a Sweetest Day gift.

Will cannot be seen
touched, heard.
Finally it cannot be known.
We follow clues . . . words,
tracked across pages
across time,
knowing they lie.

This cannot be said without a qualm.
Words do not matter *unless* bodies can love in air.

At which touchpoint do we cohere?
Bodies on fire
lose themselves,
but if they do not burn
they lose themselves
another way.
If this is a legitimate statement,
I mean, the truth,
do we need bed to support us?
Some of us love on air.

ON HEARING OF MY
DAUGHTER'S INTENDED DIVORCE

She brought you home from college
and I found you later
reading in the living room. You smiled
but didn't stand. I took a book and sat.
We read for a long time,
becoming related.

Dimly, behind your young man's bearded face,
I saw the cherub blue-eyed toddler.
Some faces hold that sweetness. "There's John
in the bunny suit with the floppy ear"
anyone would say to the dim photo—
picture child almost real as the everlasting
miracle of my daughter's newborn face.

Three years later in a northern cabin
you drank Canadian whiskey straight
and drank and vomited unhappiness you couldn't name
at the foot of a star-topped spruce.
I might have feared then, though it was years before,
to expect this news. But the good
is what is expected, is continuous,
like breath or water. All news is bad.

Your quick hands, untrained in carpentry,
made for my daughter a writing desk, a
dancing floor. For five years
I thought her time with you
stretched open as a wide embrace.
Now time's ridges touch like a closed accordion.

Between you and me there is no blood.
The air is open, unfenced space.
So it is our goodbye, too,
though we promise to "keep in touch."
May the space you travel through
be blessed, my brief son.

SUBWAY TRACKS

This was to be a poem about how Sam
loves to sit in the back seat of the subway
to watch the tracks. But where could this poem go?
Too many poems about receding tracks—
the child's golden years running away behind,
the grandmother's life running away behind.
This poem wants the front window—tracks
rushing to meet us, inevitable
and mysterious—where the motorman sits.
Delusion—like our rushing backward
to where we came, reflected in the train
that whooshes by—front tracks move exactly
like the ones behind. The only event
that counts is here inside this lighted car.
At each stop Sam says *Toot-toot. Allabooord.*
He steers by the back of the seat. Passengers
smile. He is gorgeous to look at. We lurch.
I caution him to sit. Tired of the game
he pesters, *Are we there yet?* And I name
the mundane stations of the city: Bay Street,
Bloor . . . I should beguile him with a story
but I am tired, too. We bounce lightly
over the tracks we ride on, peering
at the dark outside, the tracks we ride on
becoming the tracks behind.

BEACHES

. . . A beach like all ocean beaches,
whether polished to pebble or ground
to sand. A row of stilted cabins
grasp hands, like a chain of Boy Scouts
crossing untried streams. Several times
a day the mother stoops beside
her toddler, points to the gnashing
water as one would train a pup,
holding its nose to its feces,
points to the sun going down
like a red bathing cap. Oh, child,
nevertheless, you will wander in
until the waves lap your warm crotch.
Then you will swim far out, gulping for air.
Then you will float, white hair spinning
on the white waves. Then you will sink.
Dear, child, no obedience will save you.

GLASS HOUSES

The ladies on Scovill Road
sit right down on the toilets
at Jason's Fish House and at the Green Door Cafe
and at the Vuja Day Nite Club
they figure they got
done by the daddies
and left by the lovers
and smacked by the mothers
and robbed by the system
they figure
they have sat down in shit
and sat down in Bedlam
and sat down on emptiness
that don't flush

so what's a dose?

The houses on Scovill Road
with all the windows broke out
crouch under the high windows
of Erieview Tower—they're taller
than Erieview Tower—they see farther
than the new all glass Illuminating Company
they see piss in the doorways
and shit in the doorways
and men and women and children
doing something bad in the doorways
and soot flying over from the Flats
don't make them cry anymore. Beware
of houses with all the windows broke out
swallowing rain.

HELEN

My mother, now dead, seeing me watch the sky
for hours, would shake her head, "The child
is absent," she would say, "absent." Now I
stand at the wall watching the war—billows
of silver dust, distant shields like myriad
small suns. I do nothing. I walk about
these perfumed chambers fingering Paris'
gifts—a marble Calliope, an egg
jewelled with amethyst and emerald. My form
in the mirror surprises me always—
ivory breasts, hair like filigreed gold,
arms slender and so perfectly rounded
as if turned on a wheel. Menelaos
whispered, "Though Zeus thumb out my eyes, Helen's
beauty will be always in my sight."
Other women are ungainly, and loved.
Other women are unlovely, and loved.
Now Paris sighs, "I would bedeck the world
with mirrors, sea and sky, so that no matter
where men turn their vision will be Helen."
Unsightly crones huddle at the breakers,
chanting of the death of the bloody queen
and mighty Ilium. How strange to be
the figure of their miscast tales. Helen
and Illium belong to Zeus. This scrap
of Troy will die, and the brown mouse scratching
in its ivory wall.

THE DAY SLEEPER

You stay young until one day, perhaps
Thursday at dusk, you are silver haired
and viscid-eyed. Inside something
sputters and jams.

Friday you sleep, and sleep must feel
like flannel, for you sleep now
most days. Nights, wide-eyed, you count
your heartbeats.

You haven't attended the night
since the year of your marriage.
Now you chart the moon's silver passage
toward high piled snow.

Morning begins at the bottom
of the sky and you begin to drowse
as the lid lifts slowly and a thin
rosy glaze comforts the chair, the dresser.

You can sleep now; your wife is awake,
guarding the silver.

IN LINE

They would not have been cruel
to you, commanding, yes,
indifferent, but not brutal.
You would be among the ones
who are not quite well—
your small cough and fever—
they will pass, you think.
Perhaps that is why
all are to wash themselves—
contagion. The lines
move slowly, more than an hour.
The building you walk toward
is windowless. You hold
the soap in one hand, the hand
of your little boy
in the other. About half way
you would suddenly know
that it is not a bathhouse.
Terror seizes you,
but soon you are calm.
You lift your son
against your chilled body.
He is hot, as though
his sweet flesh would burn through
to its first soft home.
You say, *Put your head
on my shoulder, darling,
I will tell you
a story.*

THE FOX JUMPS OVER THE FENCE

. . . The fox jumps over the fence
to eat a little chicken.
Not angry. Hungry.

The chickens are too frightened
to be angry.

The farmer is angry because
he wanted to eat the chickens himself.

The farmer shoots the fox.

Now the fox should be angry,
but with a full stomach and blood
flowing quietly out of his carotid,
he is merely languid and tired.

The chicken is neither frightened nor angry.

Only the farmer,
with his steaming gun, is still angry.

I HAVE THIS HERE BIG SLEEPING BAG

Spreads out smooth as the north forty
and warm as biscuits from the oven
or the feel of goose under the feathers
when you pick it up and its squakin away
before it gets kilt for Sunday dinner.
I bring all kind of things inside there with me
like the tree layin on its side with its toes curl up
and its skinny arms over its head like to shut out
the birds and sky, like it was lonely or ashamed.
I take girls like angels, the kind you see
in picture books, with skin like a silk winda curtain
and the light shinin inside, real honey girls,
and boys with cowlicks and big teeth grinnin
too big for their face like they think you're fine
or boys like cherubs or boys like the statues
in the cemetery or town square, real handsome
put together. And I bring all kind of dogs in there
breed and strays, stringy and fat and some of 'em
still biten on a bone or a twig. And old men
when I find 'em under the bridge, spittin up blood
or spittin out teeth. Save that tooth
for the tooth fairy I tell 'em, I know a place
to put it under a pillow, and gets 'em to laugh
like crankin up an old car. The bugs and spiders
they come in by theirself, and they're runnin all over
ticklin everybody just like when cottonseed
lands on your nose or the yellowest, silkiest
hair brushes on your naked back for a minute. It can get
real active in there what with the dogs scratchin,
the old men groanin, the boys yellin, the fat women
huffin and puffin, and everyone thrashin
from the bugs. But sometimes we just lay there
on our backs lookin at the stars
or maybe one of the boys will whistle

or someone will say a word. But then all of a sudden
we hear feet machines and we know the parents are comin
again, the mothers and the fathers yankin everyone out
and shake 'em till their heads flops
back and forth like their neck is broke,
and drag 'em all the way home yellin what you think
you doin in that sleepin bag, spoonin and turnin
this way and that all together, and you
ain't even married yet!

Part II
White Smoke

DOWN IN THE ANDES

We speak of the facts of life
but facts are what erupt
at the rim of perspective.
Step to the left
and stars are closer
than they were in the sky,
thick within a bowl of blue
mountain, and the carousel
which had been the world halts
and whitens like a skull.
There was no air
except what was white
and falling.
Our skin clothed our blood
and what we thought was human
froze in our veins.
I should not speak
for the others.
Except perhaps for those
whose flesh became
my flesh; eat, they said,
eat. Or was it my dog I heard?
We were flying above this world
to hearth and home. We fell
into whiteness palpable,
vapor rising off
expanse of nothing.
We voted and covered their faces.
One could not eat. Sucking
the frozen meat he retched.
The third try he retched
his own gullet, a garden of color.
Time turned white, a held breath.
We waited for rescue, we waited for spring,

like the mountains wait, like the sky waits.
We rehearsed old jokes, old poems,
we spread our talk like a layer of leaves
over a trap.
Spring changed nothing,
blade of sun and snow
the same as it had been,
only mid-air stopped falling,
and it was spring.

We came down
from the mountain swallowing wind,
breath so putrid
we spoke only to each other's backs.
Two months the wind
howled in the dark. Now
it is tame enough to eat. The village
hunches its back in the snow,
turns from the mountains.
The people believe the stars
are whitened bones of ancestors. We know
they are chunks of meat.
I have not been hungry
for four months, less two weeks
of ravenous grace. We received
absolution. The church pondered
God's will, and concluded
God gives and God takes away
and that he gave
what he took
and took what he gave.
Life is carried warm in the mouth.
Grace before meals.
There is speech separate from man.

AT AN EXHIBIT OF HOLOCAUST ART

Shatter of flesh and bone,
florets of vein, bloodpetals
loosed as though from wedding wreaths
flung skyward. Beautiful.

Beautiful?
If flesh and bone of you?
If bone and flesh you loved?

Yes.
After time. After millennia.
Looked down upon,
looked at from beyond—
spread of flowerhead;
the rooted bleeding stump
now earth.

These are not people,
these sockets
filled with light,
ivory pelvic cradles,
not grass or trees,
this shattered
green beautiful
glass.

What does this have to do with you,
Samuel Avriham?—day old lamb
of the narrow heaving ground
of my daughter, rose petaled,
pollened with milky honey?

Millennia is far off.
The furrow is here where we kneel.
We could not rise,
we could not bear to lift our eyes,
if not to look at you,
Samuel Avriham,
barely unfurled.

PACKING LIGHT

A year later
I see black trees
encased in ice, the sky
high and steelblue,
waterfalls
between rocks
quiet as quicksilver,
like enchanted dancers,
lifted, stooped.
We walked
into and out of
brown shadows.
We chose to climb
the ice-coated gorge,
jagged, razor path
at the edge
of the millpond,
just to look,
it was so beautiful,
just to lend our bodies to the place.
We all fell many times
and one of us
spilled into the pond
and we embraced him
in our warm center
and reclothed him
with a piece from each of us
warm
off our bodies.

Five years later
the landscape
has narrowed
to just us

in a chain
across narrow ledges,
our birdcall warnings
chiming off rock,
off casements
of nightfall
shadows, patient—
nowhere to get to
but back,
the way we came.

Now
we *are* the place,
Movado Dancers
in their deep frozen bow
at the end
of the performance.
The warm, moist breath
of our huddled circle
in my lungs,
remembrance
having long ago
become body.

WAKING AT MIDNIGHT

The air's a fragrant juice, and August
ripples on the ceiling in a lace
of black oak leaves.

The dresser mirror's caught a mother of pearl flounder.
I lift my hand, and when it doesn't swim away
or flap, I slide my hand inside

as in a glove. Entrails wrap around my fingers,
a stone heart beats against my palm.

So how do I tell my feet and arms about the moon,
except to get up
and dance around the bed, around
the dresser and the mirror, appearing

and disappearing, I'm dancing through
walls.

This morning I look in the mirror
and see that I have changed.

Tonight I look up at the moon,
high in a net of stars,
and see that it has changed, too.

CONDOLENCES
for Carolyn

A week of shifting shapes,
mother and father declining on footstools,
shoeless, mourning beyond our reach;
mirrors draped to not suck out
the souls of the living hid
from us our pink skins. We kept
your catalogue seven days running.

I invoked the spirit
of the Smokey Mountains to witness
your crumpled van. I accused
the little animals, the little birds,
safe in their sanctuaries: *Where were you
when your lover, your sister died?*
—the one with the save-the-seals petitions,
save-the-eagles, and no fur,
even as glove lining?

That first year you were
my Ear of the Beyond
to whom I spoke my everyday complaints—
toothaches and unrequited loves—

and guilt.
I lived. I breathed.
I drank water and sat on my porch
to watch the rain. I held a pen
above a blank page and made my mark.

A year passed. Stone setting
and reliving the incredible phone call:
I have some very bad news for you about Carolyn she's dead.

Your death is like chains on Samson.
I want to say, Carolyn, flex!
as though by act of will you'd be here,
perhaps, across the tennis court from me.
If not there,
somewhere.

Late afternoon sunlight dances, refracted
through our atmosphere, circuits
the leaves which glow like green lightbulbs,
pierces the space between the leaves
and glides on my windows, my patio screen
as though it were tangible.
As though light were palpable.

WHITE SMOKE

Babies sleep inside their mothers
Toddlers hold their mothers' hands
And the mothers trundle to the gas chambers
In deep silence   Angels
Of the lord move
Among them humming lullabies
The eyes of all the children close
The eyes of the mothers lose their disbelief
Bitter gall pours through ducts
A cloud of souls rises from the buildings
The farmers can see the white
Smoke of souls rising from the buildings
The bodies are left on the floor
Like nightgowns of lovers
This is the holy cost
This is the holy cast
Never such peacefulness
Never such quietness
Never such deft moving of millions toward Him

WRITTEN ON CHRISTMAS EVE
*for Beth Alisha Kuby, the child of my friend David,
born November 25, 1985.*

                        Sweet child of light,
the day of your true birth
has arrived. Four short days ago darkness
swallowed most of day. Now daylight begins
to lengthen. Now darkness is only ground
so you shine brighter, and we raise our eyes

on a new morning. Crowds have come to see
the birth. Some, who expected nothing, owned
nothing till now, stare, open-mouthed, rooted
like stone as new life, small and quivering
as a barnyard mouse, finds shelter in them.

A few who felt your coming, smile, a light
like yours beginning to gather around
their heads like mist at daybreak from the earth.
Most elbow back through crowds they followed here,
push through midnight exits to different

entertainments, annoyed with the wasted
time—that all the hoopla and hosannas,
the star, the caravans of gifts, came to
only this.   They will return.

TURNING OUT

Just beyond toddling—
Mary's Caitlin, little dipper
without a handle; and Bob's
Katey, caught in the dust
of a cock and hen fight;
and baby Jesse, barely out
of the belly of the mother
who left him. All gorgeous as rosebuds
but you couldn't help
but fear for their turning out.

Over the years I got hardly more
than sound bites: Bob's gangly,
big-footed girl shooting
baskets; Mary's timid beauty
living with a carpenter;
Jesse acing high school.

Last I heard not one of them
had AIDs, not one murdered
anybody, not one calls the gutter home.
Whatever waters
they are swimming in, they are swimming.
What a testimonial . . . human spirit?
kindness of strangers? wisdom of the DNA?

or that their fearful turnings
turned into turnings toward,
turnings outward to where life is.

As for their parents and me?
I see we've turned out, too,
palms more open, necks
less stiffly settled in their yokes,
eyes showing less of the whites.

PAS DE DEUX

I am your Word
I made you, dancer,
I made you of breath
      of shadows and sunbeams
            of boundlessness

            of folding out and in like wings
      of risings and risings from the gravity of things

I am your Word,
without limb or leaving

I am the circles and spirals your body carves from air
      your twirls and leaps toward heaven
      when you most love the earth

            I was before you and will be after you
            I am the center and the circumference

I am within and within and within and within and within

I am your Dancer
I am the leap and the twirl
I am the point on the line
I am brief and desirable
I eat oranges and watch the Northward flight of geese
My being roars like oceans
I rock myself in the cradle of myself
I rock the world like my baby
I kiss the air like my lover
here and here and here
I embrace the world

I am your Dancer
I am your eyes
your mouth
your star
your tree
and something else
I am sand, river, feather, grass, moth
and I am something else
and I am something else
and I am something else

ANY DAY

From the moment you awake

Birdsong and sundawn arise

As one word.

All day kids laugh

Traffic honks A-major

And flowers grow between the crevices

Of sidewalks and up on

Every latticework and wall

As if the life of nothing depends

Upon anything.

Where?

What?

Is

The instrument of the day's humming

Like a tuning fork

Without string or key?

WHERE MARTY IS

                I lost track
after the fifteenth reunion:
Tom still not married, Al and Dave
with a team of kids in suburban houses,
wives they fell for in high school,
Marty not dead yet of cancer of the brain.
                Some say
only memory keeps the dead
alive, retrievals. I see Marty
in grey gym trunks
sinking the ball good as a pro,
or dogging his father around the yard
for something they can't afford
(actually, its tennis shoes and grass
I see), or moony-eyed with Rosemary in Study Hall,
or stuffing the crotch of his Fruit-o-the-Looms,
or charcoaling hair on his chest
for the snap of us five
pyramiding on the beach at Chippewa,
free that summer of mothers,
falling in love with anything in skirts,
mind burrs. Between us four
a great sum of Martys and misremembered Martys,
the one he alone knew, breath by breath,
fallen with him through the crack.
The sum will dwindle as one by one we join him.
                Then he is the bones of a name,
an antique watch fob, a "who's the man next to grandpa?"
                Some believe this.
                But some ask the soil,
                where are the muscle and bones of Marty?
                And some inquire of him
                in the songs of birds.

REGARDING A DEAF CHILD

Your face lies open like a field of flowers,

like a sunflower, indescribably patient,

like a sea anemone swaying in a deep tide

where only eyes answer. Can you can hear the spill

of sunlight, the moon slide across the sky, the way

you hear the pulse in your throat, the way, as in Vermeer,

sunlight and piano both are silent, both music?

I envy, at times, a world where no bullet cracks and towers

crash soundlessly as civilizations. Your world

I think is more mysterious for me than mine

for you—a symphony miles long and every

permutation listened to with hands. Your words point

to heaven, link word to flesh as nowhere but in heaven.

You drop your words into the grail of your palm,

Ten Delphic birds gather round them. Your hands skirr

above your head, saying sky! What is your silence?

For me silence is the sound that comes between sounds.

The silence moves upon the waters and it is good.

Hear it?

SPACES

Jammed in the faculty elevator,
we make ourselves tight and small
against an embarrassment of breasts,
odors intimate as underwear.
The flashing subtraction of numbers
promises quick escape. The sliding door
delivers us as from a broken anthill.

At home, I recognize my freshmen's words
on AIDS as my words, hours under
the extensor lamp, wriggling like tadpoles
in shallow water. I rest my eyes
on the darkened city whose icy
incandescence ignores my silhouette,
presents the derelict (the same one
every night?) who eats and sleeps in its eye.
Suburban stragglers huddled in their clouds
of exhalation, wait to be borne
away by the last bus before morning

down miles of glistening highway
to dispersed snowfallen houses,
carrying each other's breath
in their lungs.

LEARNING TO LOVE

You will feel lost
You will feel afraid
Empty
Not yourself.
What is missing?
was faithful as a hungry dog
comfy as aged oxfords.
What is missing?
is as though all the engines
and all the wheels
and all the motions of the wind stopped at once.
What's that? you query the silence.

Practice loving guns.
They are innocent
though they extend the reach of arms ten thousand times.
Mount them on your walls.
Pet their shining muzzles.

Practice loving potatoes.
They are innocent.
Though dust from dust
even their green eyes are innocent.

Practice loving clocks.
They are innocent.
On wrists, over hearts, on walls, in towers,
with faces round and luminous as the moon,
their whisperings,
their jubilant gongings
tell only what has come
to pass.

Wait.

NO MORE PASSION PLAYS

Let those who want
follow
pale
bleeding
feet
through stations
down valleys
of shadow
Let them
huddle
in circles
that fracture
to smaller
circles
each
lifting
a separate
hero who
points to
nebulous numina in
a distant sky

Let those who can-
not unload
their infant
selves
hoist
gibbets
Let them
set rifles on automatic
then
run

in front
Let those made passionate
by
wounds
dress
the holes

Sir
if I kiss
your tendersweet feet
when roses
run
from
them
I would
betray you

I would not
encourage with
my kisses'
balm

Each
suffering
craves
a second.

PROCESSION

Do not think of death when the weather is bad
                          —Solyag Rimpoche

1.

Her body left the weather in New York
unknown; her mother
summoned from the shining indolence
of the shore left Sarasota's weather
unknown.

Today
grey Cleveland
is shot through so with sun
the hoods of funeral cars flash
brighter than headlights.

May in November
with a March wind
swirling the fallen leaves
into golden pillars tall as men,
Sufis who whirl until the wind stops,
whirl, fragment, and lie still
until the next big gust.

2.

Never known, I imagine her
a duplicate of my daughter at, maybe, nine,
an orderly child, not one
to elbow in ahead of me.

3.

Today is May by calendar
but a few heavy flakes fall
and marble is ice to the touch.
Her fresh grave is lost
among these acres, but while I am here
I stop at another, as doing, really,
just as well.

CHOOSING YOUR GENRE

Funny about long life, when the hero
flags at the critical moment and lets
the plot get silly, tragedy, though chosen
early, not insisted on. Suffering
grows small as an obedient child,
and the good rises from the past
like a circus tiger stepping through
a smoldering hoop to the tune of
These Are a Few of My Favorite Things.
Let Anna Karenina pick herself up
from the tracks, and sail to Pennsylvania
to teach ESL to Russian immigrants
and one night dancing the Virginia Reel
fall madly in love with a farmer.
Let Billy Budd get tongue surgery
and jump ship and come finally happily
out of the closet.

AT TWO O'CLOCK IN THE NIGHT

awake
and lean on your elbow
and stare into darkness.
You will die. No getting out of it.
And your adorable son,
your joyous one, your yellow-haired
baby, whose death is impossible,
will die. And your daughter,
who has died many times
and been mourned—the one
with the two inch feet
and the one with the unbuckled
boots and misbuttoned jacket
straggling home from school,
and the one with the hippie hair
to her waistline and macrame beads—
will die. And her child,
just two years old,
who sings with his fingers
about spiders and stars.
And all the flowers,
garden varieties and wild varieties
hiding in forests, and the forests
will die, the trees at Yosemite,
older than saints.
Now in terror turn in the dark
and see beyond your ceiling,
the dying of the stars
with all their planets
and the planets with all their moons,
and the dying of the galaxies
and universe upon universe
continuing to die forever.

YOUNG SOLDIER, CLEAN AND CRISP

Tie tucked between the buttons of khakis,
delicate wrist bones exposed from starched cuffs.
By the time I met you those lovely bones
were buried in deep flesh. But here, slender
fingers gently cup a pipe, conforming
to its shape, the way a woman would want
her breast held. The photographer must have
instructed you to look away, and you
obey, with a small smile passing beyond
the brief lives of soldiers, passing beyond
your own brief beauty, beyond the future
where you will shrivel inside four hundred
pounds and finally wear out your lumbering
heart. You are not really in the picture
at all, not as you were then or ever,
but as I imagine you now to be,
somewhere smiling at this foolish earthwork.

HALFWAY HOUSE

You pretend the odor of her
Doesn't fan the hall, but hold
Your breath until your bedroom door is closed.
Someone sets an airwick on the banister.

Nothing pleases her.
Not the high room whose windows
Span an acre of apple blossoms,
A mile of goldenrod and clover

Or the earphones plugged directly into Wagner
And Brahms. Not the punctual tea
Or coddled egg or the potted
Hydrangea her son sent her

Or the fine orderliness of your concern:
Slippers together, robe folded neatly
Clothes in a footlocker under the bed.
Nothing pleases her.

Soon Brahms will play in and out of sunlight
And the open door will inhale a breeze
That's come so far it spins sea salt
On apples, and bedsheets will snap on the line,

Dazzlingly white.

THE APPOINTED PLACE

On earth Carolyn was lovely to look at,
like a sunset or the first robin.
Love at first sight
tamed her fifth grade boys.
She loved animals.
She would look into the face
of a chipmunk or a skunk
and find it sweet as infancy.
She would stand still to observe
a mosquito swelling on her thigh,
the long hike of a beetle down her arm.
Most, she loved huge, ungraceful creatures,
rhinoceroses, hippopotamuses.
She adopted a hippo at the zoo
and fed it every Sunday from her hand.

Max was a great, ungainly man who had to eat
before he ate and eat after. His fat
contained litanies of curses
for factory owners, the CIA, the FBI,
stockbrokers, generals, bank presidents—
fat cats. But he would haul his four hundred pounds
into protest marches and picket lines.
And could he sing!—the blues on Saturday nights
in saloons where they paid in drinks. Thus
he connected inside with outside,
like the lyrical blackbirds he loved—
Ella and Sarah—set free, like Billie,
the song in the vein. And though sometimes
pretty earth girls threw him peanuts, few fed him
from the delicate bowls of their hands.

                    Carolyn, meet Max.

FAKE FLOWERS

They can last longer than the longest life,
almost long as jewels—these opals and lapis,
stamped out to shine on a graveyard Flagday.

Autumn's chrysanthemums, spring-washed, are bright
as new, so not economy but love
brings these durable pastels. *Sucha pretty,*

say women in black, old poured-out Catholic
women, with backbones like kettle handles.
And they will live half life after half life,

dauntless of cycle, heavenly plastic.
Not like these rosebuds which this morning
drew blood from my finger, and rise now

from a crystal vase, composing a still life
with candlesticks and a lace tablecloth.
Already dead, we call them live flowers,

for they are still to open up wide
as a new robin. In four or five days,
they will be garbage, but already

gardens are assembling buds silken
as eyelids, clenched as newborn baby's fists,
and factories are stamping.

COME JOIN ME

on the high airing porch of my house,
come naked, no one will ask of you today,
lie face down or swaddle your eyes with cotton
and the world will quiver on your timpani, ghostly,
impalpably sweet: a small airplane
St. Margaret's noontime bells
car door front door mailbox cicadas
continuous as surf, no second, no millisecond
of silence. Listen: wheels wings buzzsaws
babies windchimes whistles mowers:
Let the world be only sound
and you will understand
that if catastrophe should blow the pieces loose,
blow them to a chaos in air,
they would be shaken
like snow in a waterglobe
where the skiers
and the wee alpine village too
are swirling particles
soon to settle down,
blown only as far as kingdom come.
Listen: the neighbor's screen door
slams with a peculiar ping,
oak leaves rustle on a high creak of branches,
in his swing, little Robbie is pumping.

INIQUITY

I live with a terrible God, a God
of impossibility, a loving
God who loves everything equally.
Who loves me unconditionally. My heart
thirsts for a just God, a God who plays
favorites, A God who selects His lovers.
But my God loves everything equally.
To Hitler he says, *My child.* To Papa
Doc Duvalier, he says, *My little one.*
They say, "God has no hands but our hands."
He loves the gunrunner and the turner
of thumbscrews. He hides their work in caves of night.
He soothes them with the silks of daylight.
On his wrist he carries a vulture.
He croons, *Caw, caw, my pretty bird.* For this
I awake at dawn in despair, and I quake
at three o'clock in the afternoon.
As a watcher in the night yearns for morning,
I yearn for a God of retribution
and anger. My God says, *Choose, my darlings.*
Every choice is right. The rich man's wolfhound
tears to pieces the mother's toddler,
He says, *Ho, my perfect child, my perfect*
puppy. For this my groin churns and I cry,
ELI, ELI, WHY? I complain, WHY? WHY?
But God's eyes are too pure to behold iniquity.

PART III
SET DOWN HERE

SET DOWN HERE

1.

When my mother bore me
she jumped
from high places, dresser tops,
the ovens of old-fashioned stoves,
trying to dislodge me.
I refused.

In due time I came
in a wash of shit and blood
covered with a motley salve—
my father's stale semen?
gloss of lubricant?

—came mum
until the cut,
the thwack.
Then I screamed.
I had expected more.

2.

Waiting
on a low, three-legged stool,
keeping books: in the black,
short columns of one of this
and two of that, hard, small,
reassuring. In the red, owed or owing,
something unknown, that I love.

3.

Spurt of lilac, chirps
of grey-brown birds
like stiletto heels on dawn,
movement of the big toe—
if these were mine forever
addiction might find forever
long enough.

4.

At the instant of waking, panic.
Mind's spaceless falling latches
to day, to hour, holds there
at a godless angle
reciting the Withouts.
Coffee, cigarettes, bring me about.

5.

Kneeling at the side of my house,
the strip of garden
with dawn to dusk sunlight
that separates
my lot from my neighbors,
I lifted my eyes from my weeding
to the familiar houses, lawns,
lampposts, sidewalks,
etched as the world that is
into my eyeballs, perfect
replication of the moment before,
suddenly strange, floating
like a scene returned to
from a long time away,
and a voice said,
You are not from this place.

6.

Then from where?

7.

When the guest on the late night talk show
explained that the word *disaster*
means catastrophe among the stars
I surprised myself
with sudden weeping,
there in the parking lot,
with the guest droning on and on,
with the insects and tree frogs of September
hurrying their gratings
as though fortissimo would forestall October,
with a few windows in the thousand-
suited high-rise still incandescent
or fluorescent and the freeway
moving in its battery lights
like an endless train—invented lights
for this inky globe.

8.

The sorrow I speak of
is not my sorrow.
It is the dirge
of particulate matter,
the moan of the calendar.
I do not own
this sorrow.

9.

Death sound is different
from birth sound.

Death chortles or gurgles,
grates cricket thighs
across blackboards.
Birth practices the first scales
of the soprano,
the high breaking hoot
of the wolf, reveille of ram's horn and conch—
octaves of animals and animal parts
blasting into the beyond
We are not from this place.

10.

Hoot of the baby in the chalice:
raise a toast with this baby,
little piss hardon
squirting
pediatrician and priest,
baptismal font,
fruit of the womb
on the tongue.

Golden shadows when the baby's startled eyes,
reaching their sunset,
bisect the given.
It had always expected more,
even after fish stories
about sunken Atlantis,
how they swam through marble
pillars as though it were an aquarium,
swam through golden hair
and golden bodies.

11.

In the AIDS ward
of the maximum security prison
the inmates feed
each other with spoons,
stroke each other's fevered
shriveling foreheads,
croon lullabies
to each other's addicted fetal bodies—
Hush, little cutthroat,
don't say a word,
Papa's gonna buy you
a grey-brown bird.

12.

The heaving pelvis hove the baby to a colder climate
where angst beats in the fontanel,
and all continents
perpetually drift
to colder climates. That *is*
the drift: one tallies
the black and the red
and stays put in the scale of things
or jumps.

13.

The baby,
born from heat into cold,
from zero toward zero,
with one eye pressed against
the dome of the mother
and the other eye opened
on the flickering world,
begins to keep books.

It studies how to be at home here,
earnestly looks for lessons:
the grey-brown birds, tiny Atlases.
seem to have the answer,
as do the lilacs,
and the clouds, forming
and reforming as though they
had nothing to lose, and the sea,
caressing itself, striding
upon its own waves, laying down
upon itself.

14.

What can it be but pain,
the harsh dissonance
rising off the hills
of Colorado, of Spain, of Poland
where, they believe, humans become
the long hair and the flesh-eating stomach,
the plaintiff wail we recognize
and shudder to and sub-vocalize.
We know it means
I had expected more.
I am not from this place.

And yet the stiff grasses,
the coupling in warm sand,
the standing haunch to comforting haunch,
the limbs enticed to their utmost span
by the perfume of rodent,
the red eyes etched with changing moons,
closed as if in bliss
as the head lifts to blast its howl,
might be enough
if it were forever.

15.

The baby all its life
snorts the world,
mainlines it,
holds it under its tongue,
blends it and fries it,
becomes addicted
to the push and pull of moons
that sometimes lie soft and golden
as the dome of the mother on the horizon,
to music so constant
it is not heard,
like the voices of mother and father
on days they are happy
drowsing into the baby's room
like a silk coverlet.

16.

I live in a trance of clouds,
my heart moves
when the wind
bends over the grass
trance of the grape
round and smooth on the tongue
like spurt of lilac.

Fiesta in the barrio
Movement of the big toe
Chiaroscuro of the dungeon
The bliss.

www.ingramcontent.com/pod-product-compliance
Lightning Source LLC
Chambersburg PA
CBHW020920090426
42736CB00008B/719